Totally Crazy for Horses

Karen Briggs

and

Shawn Hamilton

Scholastic Canada Ltd.
Toronto New York London Auckland Sydney
Mexico City New Delhi Hong Kong Buenos Aires

Azteca

When the Spanish Conquistadors invaded Central America and seized the native peoples' lands and treasures in the 1500s, the secret of their success was the horse. The people living there had never seen such magnificent and fearsome animals, and thought the Spaniards must be gods.

The horses brought to the New World in the Spanish ships had been bred for centuries not only for war, but also to be used in bullfighting. They had grace and elegance, and they also had "cow sense," which proved to be very useful when the conquerors began to set up cattle ranches, called *haciendas*, all over New Spain. These horses became the ancestors of many breeds in North and South America, including the American Quarter Horse, a favourite cowhorse of today's ranchers and cattlemen, and the tough little Criollo, used as a saddle horse throughout Central and South America.

In 1972, horse breeders in Mexico decided they wanted to recreate the original Spanish-style horse of the *charros* (Mexican cowboys), by crossing noble Spanish Andalusians with sensible, cattle-savvy Quarter Horses and hardy Criollos. They called this cross the Azteca, the National Horse of Mexico.

Elegant, athletic Aztecas are now becoming popular throughout the Americas. They are naturally balanced and athletic, enabling them to leap sideways in the blink of an eye to avoid the horns of a bull, or to perform the delicate movements of dressage. Yet they have a very loving, mellow temperament and are intelligent and easy to train. Like their Andalusian ancestors, many Aztecas are grey in colour, though they may also be palomino, buckskin, chestnut or bay. Only solid colours are permitted in Mexico, but in the United States, Aztecas of all patterns and markings are accepted for registration.

Aztecas are slow to mature, but are very sound and durable, with hooves as hard as iron. They stand from 14:2 to 16 hands tall, a compact size which makes them easy to mount and dismount several times a day during the course of ranch work. Although the Azteca is a new breed, it is already popular not only with *charros*, but with Mexican bullfighters called *rejoneros*, with dressage riders and ropers, and even with showjumpers. With such a fine combination of beauty and brains, their dancing hooves will surely leave their mark in many more arenas in the future.

Fast Fact

The first registered Azteca was a stallion called Casarejo, whose sire was a Spanish stallion and whose dam was a Quarter Horse. Today, registered Aztecas may be any combination of Andalusian, Quarter Horse and Criollo blood, as long as the Criollo makes up no more than a quarter of their ancestry and they are at most five-eighths Andalusian or Quarter Horse.

Selle Français

Some say it is the wonderful grass that grows in Normandy that has helped make the Selle Français such an exceptional breed for showjumping and dressage. Others say it's the special blend of bloodlines from many of the most athletic horses in the world. Either way, the Selle Français is the pride of France and the mount of most of the country's top riders!

The Selle Français was developed in the 1800s by crossing English Thoroughbreds, native French mares and the most athletic horses used for driving, such as the Norfolk Trotter. Two types of horses resulted from this breeding program — the speedy French Trotter, still used today for harness racing, and the Anglo-Norman (a name indicating a cross of English and French bloodlines), which was preferred as a saddle horse. Later, to reflect the results of the national breeding program, the Anglo-Norman was renamed *le cheval de selle français*, meaning the French saddle horse.

Today the Selle Français is internationally renowned as a showjumper. At the 2002 World Equestrian Games in Jerez, Spain, France won the team gold medal for showjumping with all four of its members mounted on Selle Français stallions. Another Selle Français stallion, Baloubet du Rouet, is the only horse to have won the World Cup of showjumping three times in a row (1998—2000) with Brazilian rider Rodrigo Pessoa in the irons. This superbly athletic breed is also winning ribbons in the dressage arena and in the sport of three-day eventing.

Like many other European breeds, the Selle Français is considered a warmblood — but infusions of Thoroughbred, Arabian and French Trotter blood make him a faster and more sensitive horse than many other warmbloods. That's just fine with French riders, who prefer a horse who must be ridden with finesse and elegance rather than muscle. But the Selle Français is also known for having a willing attitude and great affection for people. Selle Français are tall, from 15:2 to 17 hands, and resemble large-boned Thoroughbreds, with finely sculpted heads, long elegant necks and a streamlined look. They are most often chestnut, but can be any colour. Horses approved for breeding wear a brand on their flank that looks like a six-pointed star with the letters SF in the middle.

Fast Fact In France, Selle Français horses can be found on the racetrack as well as the showjumping arena. They race in their own division, called the AQPSA (*autre que pur sang* association, meaning "other than Thoroughbred").

Belgian Warmblood

For many centuries, most of the horses in beautiful Belgium were the massive type who plowed fields and pulled beer wagons. But today, many horses from Belgium are soaring high in the air!

The Belgian Warmblood is a new breed, one that excels in the showjumping ring. It was developed in the 1950s, when a number of different bloodlines of showjumping and dressage horses from across Europe were combined. Breeding "hot" (Arabian or Thoroughbred) blood to "cold" (draft horse) creates what is known as a "warmblood"— and an ideal mix of speed and strength. In Belgium, this combination resulted in a tall, powerful horse with tremendous athletic ability.

To see just how talented Belgian Warmbloods are, you need look no further than the most famous representative of the breed — Big Ben, the superstar partner of "Captain Canada," Ian Millar.

Although he was purchased as a youngster in Holland, Big Ben was a Belgian Warmblood through and through. Standing 17:3 hands tall, with a big, awkward looking head, he was not the most beautiful of creatures, but when he was in the jumping arena he seemed to fly without wings. Ben and Ian were the first partnership to win back-to-back showjumping World Cup Finals in 1988 and 1989, becoming Canadian national heroes in the process. They also represented Canada at three consecutive Olympic Games, the 1986 World Championships and the 1987 Pan American Games, and racked up over forty Grand Prix victories — making Big Ben the top showjumper in Canadian history.

"Bennie" is not alone in his accomplishments, of course. In showjumping competition at the 1996 Olympics in Atlanta, Georgia, there were 10 Belgian Warmbloods representing 7 different nations! An increasing number of them are also winning in the dressage arena.

Over 4000 Belgian Warmblood foals are born every year, and stallions and mares are carefully inspected before they can be used for breeding. That way, only the very best individuals pass on their traits to the next generation. All foals born in the same year are named with the same letter of the alphabet. For example, all Belgian Warmbloods foaled in 2003 have names beginning with the letter D, those in 2004 with the letter E, and for 2005 it's the letter F.

Fast Fact

Another famous Belgian Warmblood was Jus de Pomme (Apple Juice). At the 1996 Olympic Games, with rider Ulrich Kirchhoff, he won both the individual and team gold medals in showjumping for Germany.

Camargue

In ancient myths, the great sea-god Neptune rose out of the ocean driving a chariot pulled by white horses, whose waving manes made up the sea spray on the waves.

You can imagine you're seeing the living descendants of Neptune's horses in the Camargue region of southeastern France, where the Rhone river fans out as it meets the sea. Grazing peacefully in the marshes and the dunes, co-existing with ibises, pink flamingos and herds of fierce black bulls, the "white horses of the sea" live wild most of the year. Ankle-deep in water, swept by harsh north winds called the Mistral in winter, and patiently enduring intense sun and biting insects in summer, they have been there as long as anyone can remember. Historical records suggest that Camargue horses may have been used to pull chariots in the Roman circus, over two thousand years ago. Some say the proof of their existence goes back much further, to the famous 17,000-year-old Lascaux cave paintings. These ancient figures depict horses that look remarkably similar to modern-day Camargues.

Born dark, all Camargue horses gradually turn grey by the age of four or five. They are stocky and pony-sized, averaging around 13:3 hands, with thick necks and unusually small ears. Their short, sturdy legs and extra-hard hooves are adapted to wading in the marsh. They have black skin, which helps protect them from sunburn in the summer, and their calm, almost lazy attitudes are their way of conserving energy in their harsh environment. Camargue horses are experts in survival, managing with very little help from humans by grazing on the salty marsh grasses and reeds and browsing on the leaves of bushes.

These days, all Camargue horses are privately owned, and sport brands on their haunches to identify them. But they still live undisturbed most of the year, except for those used as riding horses by the *gardians*, the cowboys of the Camargue. Because Camargue horses share their habitat with the wild cattle of the region, they are the perfect mounts for rounding up these rather skittish and temperamental beasts. The *gardians* even use a cattle prod that looks like Neptune's trident!

Most Camargue horses are now protected and live in the Camargue Regional Nature Park, which was established in 1927 to help preserve their habitat. There are very few Camargue horses outside of France, but the breed has a few fans and breeders in Italy, England and Belgium.

Fast Fact

Traditional Camargue saddles have very high pommels and cantles, and are extremely comfortable, but even so, the cowboys of the Camargue rarely ride their horses at a trot. Camargue horses have an extremely pleasant walk and canter, but their gait at the trot is usually short, choppy and — according to those who've ridden them — best avoided altogether!

Caspian

The beautiful Caspian looks like a delicate, miniature china sculpture of a horse. But they're a lot tougher than they look! In the most remote of mountain ranges in northern Iran, they have survived centuries of civil war, famine and hardship. Until the 1960s, no one really knew how rare or how important they were.

Their numbers had dwindled to fewer than 50 individuals when Louise Firouz, an American woman living in Iran with her husband Narcy, stumbled across a pony hitched to a very heavy cart in the town of Amol in 1965. She described him as "a small, slim bay stallion; a perfect small horse, with a bright glossy coat, slim legs, tiny hooves, and the body and carriage of a well-bred oriental horse — no shaggy pony this, but an eleven-hand dream out of a Russian fairy tale."

Louise Firouz was searching for small mounts for the children in her riding school, and she found them in the animals she named Abscheh Kazar, or Caspian ponies, after the nearby Caspian Sea. The horse she had found and purchased, Ostad, became a wonderful mount for her students, and she set out to look for more horses like him in the cotton fields and rice paddies around Amol. She soon discovered that they were extremely rare. Worse, those she did find were often starving and suffering from lack of veterinary care. She rescued every animal she could and began to breed them at her riding school. And as she researched the history of the horses, she became convinced that the Caspian was the ancient and pure breed shown in Persian carvings from many centuries ago. Most people had thought these horses to be extinct for the last thousand years!

Despite Caspians' small size, many people believe that they are more like horses than ponies. Their slim dimensions mean that they are easy for small children to ride, and they are very trainable and gentle with children. They make superb jumpers and driving ponies. They come in all sorts of solid colours, and stand only about 9 to 12 hands high.

Caspians are still very rare. Louise Firouz has worked with the Iranian government to establish a national breeding program, but war has broken out on several occasions and each time the government has taken the horses away. Fortunately, she has also sent several Caspians to Great Britain and the United States, where a few dedicated breeders are working to increase their numbers. There are still fewer than 1000 Caspians in the world.

Fast Fact

Many people believe that the Caspian is the ancestor of the Arabian. Both genetic and archaeological evidence show many similarities, including the prominent almond-shaped eyes, a high-set tail and a dished face.

Gelderlander

The people of the Netherlands (also known as Holland) love their horses, and have developed a number of popular breeds, including the handsome jet-black Friesian and the powerful and athletic Dutch Warmblood. But have you ever heard of the Gelderlander?

This large horse with the high-stepping trot is an elegant carriage horse that originated in the province of Gelderland, located in the middle of the Netherlands. His ancestry comes from crossing the native mares of the region with many types of successful driving horses from other parts of Europe. The Hackney and the Norfolk Roadster from England contributed to the Gelderlander's bloodlines, as did the Holsteiner and the Oldenburg from Germany, the Andalusian from Spain, and the Anglo-Norman from France, just to name a few.

In the north of Holland, sticky clay soils required a large, powerful horse to pull a plow or vehicle through the mud. But farther south, in Gelderland, the soil is sandy, so the horses who developed there have a lighter frame and a more energetic way of going — which makes them eye-catching when hitched to a polished and shiny carriage.

Unlike many of the other breeds featured in this book, the history of the Gelderlander goes back only about a hundred years. His bloodlines are carefully recorded and controlled by the Dutch National Studbook called the KWPN, which also registers Dutch Warmblood riding horses and a third breed, the Dutch Harness Horse (which resembles the British Hackney).

Gelderlanders come in most colours, including pinto, with chestnut and grey being the most common. They usually stand between 15:2 and 16 hands tall. They often have flashy white markings on their faces and legs. Their heads may best be described as plain, sometimes sporting a Roman nose, and they have longish bodies and shortish legs. But Gelderlanders also have beautifully arched necks and powerful hindquarters. They are becoming known for their jumping ability as well as their talents in harness!

Fast Fact

Every year, on the second Saturday of August, the National Day of the Gelderlander Horse is held in Hengelo, the Netherlands. Dozens of stallions and mares of all ages are presented in harness and under saddle, both in the dressage ring and the showjumping arena, for both breeders and the public to admire.

Gotland

On the wooded island of Gotland, in the Baltic Sea off the coast of Sweden, lives a mysterious pony the native islanders call *skogsbaggar*, which means "forest ram." His other name, in Swedish, is *Russ*, which comes from the Old Norse term, *hross*. In the English-speaking world we know him as the Gotland pony, and his origins are indeed puzzling.

Gotland ponies are often referred to as a living relic of the Stone Age. They show many of the same primitive characteristics as the ancient wild breed of horse, the Tarpan, who some think is the ancestor of almost all breeds of modern horses. No one is sure whether Gotlands made their own way to the island or were brought by humans, many centuries ago. But they made a home for themselves in the Swedish forests and survived many a harsh winter, until the middle of the 1800s, when farmers started building fences across the land, reducing the amount of food available to the ponies. By the beginning of the 20th century, only about 150 Gotland ponies were left, and during the desperate days of World War I (1914—1918), starving soldiers and civilians were forced to kill many of the animals for meat.

Fortunately, when the war ended, Gotland farmers took action to save their native ponies. They gathered up eight ponies who had survived and established a little breeding herd on a winter pasture of about 80 hectares. These eight formed the basis for the revival of the Gotland breed. Today there are about 9000 Gotland ponies in Sweden, and they are also popular in Denmark, Finland and other parts of Europe.

In North America, Gotlands are still not well known, but they are increasing in popularity as people discover how versatile they are.

Gotland ponies are usually black, bay, dun or chestnut in colour, and stand between 11:2 and 13 hands. Though small, they are strong enough to carry an adult rider, and are known for their athletic talents. They are clever jumpers and speedy trotters, often used in Sweden for harness racing at the trot. They have a very friendly, cooperative disposition, which also makes them ideal all-round ponies for kids.

Fast Fact

If you visit the island of Gotland, you might be lucky enough to spot some Gotland mares and foals in their protected forest habitat. Their dark coats help to camouflage them in the foliage, but if you are very still and patient, you might see them materialize as if by magic from the shadows!

Irish Draught

From Ireland, where the sport of showjumping originated, comes the Irish Draught (pronounced "draft"). Despite his name, he is not a true draft horse, but an athlete and a jumper like no other!

Hundreds of years ago, Irish farmers had less need for a heavy draft horse than farmers in England or Scotland. Instead, they needed a medium-weight "all-rounder" horse who could work the land but also trot smartly when hooked to a cart, or go fox-hunting on the weekends. The ideal Irish horse was one who could go all day and jump anything he faced. And what he often faced was stone walls nearly 2 metres high!

The horses who excelled at all of these jobs were handsome, free-moving animals with great stamina and a solid, sturdy build, though not as heavy as that of a draft horse. Today's Irish Draughts stand quite tall, often topping 16 hands. They come in any solid colour (greys are especially common), and have extremely sound limbs, tough feet and an almost uncanny jumping ability.

Not only are Irish Draughts world-renowned for their boldness and bravery, they are prized for being "easy keepers" too — they can survive and thrive on very little feed. A couple of hundred years ago, the diet of an Irish Draught horse might have consisted of chopped gorse (a tough, spiny shrub), bran and boiled turnips!

Today, Irish Draught blood is much sought after as it adds athleticism, substance, common sense and bravery to other breeds of horses, especially the Thoroughbred. Irish Draught—Thoroughbred crosses, sometimes called Irish Sport Horses, are some of the world's top showjumpers and three-day eventers. In fact, the Irish Draught is so popular as a cross with other breeds that purebred Irish Draughts are now somewhat hard to find. Today there are fewer than 2000 worldwide, but The Irish Horse Board is now making a concerted effort to preserve the valuable bloodlines.

Fast Fact Cagney, an Irish Sport Horse by the Irish Draught stallion Clover Hill, represented Canada on many occasions in the international showjumping ring in the 1990s, with rider Eric Lamaze.

Cleveland Bay

Which carriage horse is preferred by Queen Elizabeth II? It's the Cleveland Bay, the oldest breed of horse to have originated in the British Isles. The breed is now coming back from the brink of extinction, thanks in part to the efforts of Her Majesty, who has bred these striking animals since the 1960s.

Cleveland Bays hail from the Cleveland area of northern Yorkshire. They are thought to have originated in the 1600s, when breeders crossed big bay-coloured local mares with Arabian and Barb stallions. Similar crossbreedings resulted in another famous breed, the Thoroughbred. But while the Thoroughbred was intended for speed, the Cleveland Bay's destiny was as a durable, handsome and versatile carriage and riding horse.

He was originally known as the "Chapman's horse," because travelling merchants who favoured this type of horse were sometimes called chapmen. But in the 1880s, the first studbook recording the breed's bloodlines dubbed him the Cleveland Bay, because his colour is always bay. (Only a small star on the forehead is permitted.)

From very early on, with no additional bloodlines from other breeds, the Cleveland Bay "bred true" — all of the members of the breed resemble each other very closely in colour, size, conformation and disposition.

This makes them easy to match up when you want to drive a team of horses, and simple to distinguish from other breeds.

Cleveland Bays fell out of favour when cars and tractors replaced them for transportation and farm work, but their strength and power made them excellent army horses, pulling heavy artillery in World War I. Many were killed in action. By the early 1960s, fewer than 10 mature Cleveland Bay stallions were known to exist. That was when Queen Elizabeth II stepped in, purchasing a stallion named Mulgrave Supreme. He sired 16 sons and helped replenish the breed, but there are still fewer than 650 purebred Cleveland Bays in England and North America.

The Cleveland Bay is first and foremost a carriage horse, but he is also wonderful for sports such as fox-hunting, where his sturdy build and wonderful jumping ability come in handy! It is said there is no better horse for a day's hunting in heavy mud. The Cleveland Bay has a steady, sensible disposition, though some people think he has a stubborn streak. He is still very popular for crossbreeding with the Thoroughbred, adding soundness and strength. Many Olympic showjumpers, dressage horses, and three-day eventers have been Thoroughbred–Cleveland Bay crosses.

Fast Fact

William Cody, the legendary cowboy known as Buffalo Bill, imported several Cleveland Bays from England to use as ranch horses!

The Camargue

Camargues are
sometimes called
" white horses
of the sea. "

Kiger Mustang

Mustangs, the free-running horses who roam the North American West, come in all shapes, sizes and colours. That's because they're a mixture of all of the different breeds brought to the continent when Europeans decided to settle there. There were draft horses for pulling stumps and plowing fields, high-stepping trotters to pull carriages, ponies to work in the mines, and finest of all, the noble Spanish-bred chargers who were saddle horses for the earliest invaders, the Conquistadors. All of these bloodlines mingled when horses were turned loose or escaped into the wild.

In a few places, however, the Mustangs have an undeniable resemblance to the Spanish Sorraia (the ancient ancestor of the Andalusian and the Lusitano) of centuries ago. Three such bands were found in 1977, in a remote high desert area of Oregon called Beaty Butte. Small but powerful in build, they were all dun in colour, ranging from very pale to mousy brown, with dorsal stripes running down their spines and pale zebra-like stripes on their legs — markings which indicated their primitive origins. Their luxuriant tails were black with lighter hairs on the sides, a colouration called "tail frosting." Their faces and conformation looked like the Sorraia's, too.

The people from the Oregon Bureau of Land Management (BLM), who had rounded up these mustangs, knew they had discovered something special. They sent blood samples to experts at the University of Kentucky, who found that these feral (wild) horses were indeed related to the old Spanish chargers.

The BLM decided that these special Mustangs should be preserved, so they placed the herds in the Kiger Herd Management Area in Oregon, near Kiger Gorge, and made sure there were no other horses in the area. Every four years, the herds are rounded up and some young horses may be put up for adoption.

Despite having lived for centuries without knowing the touch of humans, Kiger Mustangs are easily trained and show great stamina and cow sense, just like their Spanish ancestors. This places them much in demand as ranch horses. Their hardiness, intelligence and beauty are also preserved by a few private breeders in Canada and the United States.

Fast Fact The fiery stallion depicted in the animated movie *Spirit: Stallion of the Cimarron* was based on a handsome buckskin Kiger Mustang named Donner.

Lipizzan

You may have heard of the mythical flying horse called Pegasus . . . but have you heard of the horse who can fly without wings?

The Lipizzan (or Lipizzaner as it is sometimes called) is a dressage specialist. In the indoor arena at the Spanish Riding School in Vienna, Austria, Lipizzans glide across the sand with authority and grace, to the delight of the galleries of people watching from above. But they are one of the few breeds in the world who also perform the "Airs Above the Ground": movements like the *courbette*, the *ballotade* and the *capriole*, which once upon a time were used to intimidate the enemy in warfare. When a Lipizzan leaps into the air, unleashing his tremendous power, he almost seems to take flight.

The Lipizzan takes his name from the town of Lipizza, which is now in Slovenia. At a stud established there over 400 years ago, the breed was developed by crossing Spanish Andalusians with Italian and Arabian horses. All Lipizzans descend from six foundation stallions, and wear a brand to show which "sire line" they belong to. Conversano, Favory, Maestoso, Neapolitano, Pluto or Siglavy.

For hundreds of years, the best Lipizzan stallions were chosen to perform at the Spanish Riding School in Vienna, while the mares were favoured for pulling coaches. The breed's existence has often been threatened by war. After World War I, with the foundation herd scattered, the state stud was moved from Lipizza to the Austrian town of Piber, where it still exists today.

During World War II, many of the horses were captured by Nazi Germany. When this herd was endangered by the advance of the Russian army, a dramatic rescue was staged by the United States cavalry, led by General George Patton. The Lipizzan stallions, mares and foals were smuggled out of Austria — disguised, at times, with oil and wax to darken their coats. Ten years after the war ended, they were able to perform once again at the beautiful Spanish Riding School, which had miraculously survived the bombing of Vienna.

Lipizzans are slow to mature, but can live up to 35 years. It is said that it takes 8 years to train one to perform at the Spanish Riding School . . . but a lifetime for a rider to learn to ride one! The Lipizzan's natural balance and lively gaits, combined with his loyalty and common sense, make the process a joy.

Fast Fact

Almost all Lipizzans are born black and gradually turn white as they mature. But occasionally a Lipizzan of another colour — usually bay or buckskin — is born, and these horses are especially prized. Superstition says that Austria will have fallen on hard times when a "coloured" horse is not included in the Spanish Riding School performances.

Lusitano

From Portugal comes the proud and noble Lusitano, a horse as skilled in the bullfighting ring as he is in the more gentle art of dressage.

He and his close cousin, the Andalusian, who hails from across the border in Spain, have influenced countless other breeds of horses, including the Lipizzan, the Cleveland Bay, the Irish Draught, the Welsh Cob, the Mustang, the Friesian and the Hanoverian. And he has made a huge hoofprint on history as well. Once known as the Iberian, he was the favoured mount of Roman soldiers, was praised by the ancient Greek horseman Xenophon (who wrote one of the first textbooks on horsemanship), and strode into battle in the Crusades in the 12th century with King Richard the Lionheart. Some say he is the most ancient breed of saddle horse in the world, with a story that reaches back over 5000 years.

With his compact frame, powerful arched neck, and low, rounded croup, the Lusitano is built for power and agility rather than speed. He can crouch like a cat and turn on a dime — qualities which help him dance just out of reach of the sharp horns of Portuguese bulls while thousands of spectators cheer. Those same talents make him a favoured partner for the art of classical dressage, for he is particularly skilled at movements such as the *piaffe* (a trot-on-the-spot), which requires great strength and collection. The Lusitano has what is often called a natural *joie de vivre*, which gives him great stage presence, and unusual intelligence, which makes him a pleasure to train.

Lusitanos have heads with a Roman profile — dignified, rather than pretty! They often have long, flowing manes and tails, and luxuriant forelocks that may reach their nostrils. Lusitanos come in many solid colours, but are most often grey or black, and stand between 14:3 and 15:3 hands.

Fast Fact

The Lusitano loves to be in the spotlight! With his natural grace and proud bearing, he is the breed favoured by many circuses — including Cavalia, a spectacular show that features 13 beautiful Lusitano stallions performing under saddle and "at liberty."

Marwari

The mysterious, exotic Marwari is a horse with a warrior heritage. He was bred for warfare by the Rathores, a tribe living in Marwar, a desolate and harsh region of Rajasthan in India. His distinctive ears, which curve inwards like the steel blade of a scimitar, echo his warrior heritage.

Since the 1200s, the Marwari has been known as "the horse of the Maharajas" (the kings and emperors of ancient India). So prized were these horses that they were declared to be superior to humans, and only the highest-ranking cavalry officers and nobles were allowed to own or ride them. Many ancient texts celebrate their bravery and cleverness in battle, describing them as "bred to lift the heart in battle and please the eye."

Not only are Marwari horses fearless, they have amazing stamina and can travel long distances in the desert with a minimum of food and water. Many a rider's life has been saved by the renowned Marwari homing instinct, which enables these horses to come home safely when lost in the desert. And those unusual ears, which sometimes touch at the tips, are said to give him exceptional powers of hearing, to warn both horse and rider of approaching danger even from a long way away.

Today, Marwaris are prized as energetic, athletic mounts, with a strong competitive streak. In India they are used for polo, jumping, dressage and especially endurance riding. Despite the fact that they are short-strided — because that is the most efficient way of moving in the sand of their native region — Marwaris are very comfortable to ride. They stand between 14 and 17 hands, and come in all colours; pintos, called Ablaks, are especially favoured.

Fast Fact

The region of Marwar is now called Jodhpur, which is also the source behind the name of a certain style of English riding pants. No wonder horses are a way of life there!

Missouri Fox Trotter

When ballroom dancing, humans sometimes glide across the floor in a smooth and graceful dance called the fox trot. But few human fox trot enthusiasts know that they are simply imitating a horse!

The Missouri Fox Trotter is the breed that glides. Fox Trotters are known for their wonderfully silky, sure-footed gait, which carries them easily over bumpy terrain while their riders sit almost motionless in the saddle. To perform the fox trot, Missouri Fox Trotters walk with their front legs and trot with their back legs, gliding the hind feet forward to make the gait as smooth as glass. Keeping the rhythm with their nodding heads and swinging tails, they can perform this gait for hours without tiring.

The breed, and the gait, are thought to take their name from an important stallion named Old Fox, who passed along his gentle disposition, his stamina and his soundness to his foals. These were all important qualities to the pioneer families who settled the rugged, forest-covered Ozark Mountains of Missouri in the early 1800s. And they're just as important today for riders who enjoy long-distance trail riding, a sport at which the Missouri Fox Trotter excels. Most of the people who own Missouri Fox Trotters use them for trail and pleasure riding, rather than showing. United States forest rangers, who often patrol huge areas of wild territory in America's national parks, also appreciate the ground-covering gait of the Missouri Fox Trotter, and know they can be depended on to carry a rider safely through treacherous terrain.

Missouri Fox Trotters stand between 14 and 16 hands and are sturdily built to carry a large rider if necessary. But their temperament is so quiet and gentle that Fox Trotters are also suitable for children, and often make great horses for beginners.

They come in a number of beautiful colours, including pinto, perlino, champagne and, rarely, silver dapple – a dark, dusky body with lighter dapples and an almost silver mane and tail.

Fast Fact

Like many other American breeds, the Missouri Fox Trotter has many influences running through his veins. The Arabian, the Thoroughbred, the Canadian and the Morgan contributed elegance and stamina, while the American Saddlebred, the Standardbred and the Tennessee Walker all helped to create his unique fox-trotting gait.

Przewalski's Horse

The Przewalski's horse (pronounced "serve-ow-ski" or "sha-val-ski") is the last truly wild species of horse. If it's not running free on the cold and windswept steppes of Mongolia, it's probably in a zoo, where breeding programs are working to bring the breed back from the brink of extinction.

Przewalski's horse got its name from Russian explorer Colonel Nikolai Przewalski, who spotted these rare wild horses in Mongolia and China in 1881. But the colonel wasn't the first European to witness these unusual animals. A travel journal written by a Scottish doctor in the early 1700s has an accurate description of horses that were small and dun-coloured, with brushy upright manes, dorsal stripes along their spines, zebra-like markings on their legs, donkey-like tails, oatmeal-coloured muzzles, and no forelocks. They looked remarkably like prehistoric cave paintings of horses, from an age when the animal was a source of meat rather than a tame companion.

As human populations continued to expand across Europe and Asia from the 1500s to the 1700s, the shy Przewalski's horses had fewer and fewer places where they could live in peace. By the 19th century the herds were all gone . . . or so people thought until Col. Przewalski made several journeys to the most remote regions of Mongolia and brought back a skull and a horsehide, proof that a few herds of the wild horses still survived near the edge of the Gobi Desert.

Przewalski's horses were a source of great curiosity among Europeans, and a few who liked to collect and keep rare animals wanted them for their collections. Expeditions were organized to capture some of the horses, but the wily animals eluded them every time. The most determined hunters decided to try to capture foals, four of which arrived at Frederic von Falz-Fein's estate in southern Russia in 1899. Soon, more Przewalski's horses were placed in zoos in Europe and the United States, but they refused to be tamed or trained, and suffered great hardship during their journeys. Many died. As a result, all of the captive Przewalski's horses seen in zoos today have descended from the 13 who survived.

No herds of wild Przewalski's horses have been seen in Mongolia since 1969. But a project begun in 1977 is now gradually re-introducing them to the wild. A cooperative breeding program among many different zoos is helping to bring population numbers back up, and some of the horses have been moved to large reserves to help them learn to live on their own again. About 60 were released on the steppes of Mongolia in the late 1990s, and it is hoped that, with government protection, they will once again run free and wild in their native country.

Fast Fact

Though there has been much debate about the issue, researchers have now determined through genetics that Prezwalski's Horse is probably a separate species from domestic horses, the way donkeys or zebras are.

National Show Horse

The flashy, high-stepping American Saddlebred is often called "the peacock of the show ring." And the graceful, hot-blooded Arabian has had his beauty and intelligence praised in prose and poetry for centuries. So what would you get if you combined the best qualities of these two outstanding breeds? You'd get the National Show Horse, a horse with charisma to spare!

Though Arabian—Saddlebred crosses have been popular for many years, the name "National Show Horse" was only adopted in the early 1980s, when legendary trainer Gene Lacroix and other fans of these horses helped to found a registry to promote the new breed. They wanted to encourage breeders to produce horses who were versatile and fun family mounts, able to perform in many different disciplines.

National Show Horses can be any combination of Arabian and Saddlebred, as long as they are at least 25 percent Arabian. They should have the Arabian's beauty, soundness and stamina as well as the Saddlebred's high-stepping action, graceful swan neck and show-ring sparkle.

National Show Horses sometimes inherit the Saddlebred's "extra gears" — the slow gait and the rack, which they perform in addition to walking, trotting and cantering.

In the show ring, National Show Horses love to strut their stuff. Some classes at a NSH event reward the horses with the flashiest, most high-stepping trot, while others give ribbons to those with a smooth, gentle way of going and flawless manners.

National Show Horses can be shown in harness or under Western tack, or in English "saddle-seat" attire, complete with bowler hats and boutonnieres for the riders! Every year there is a thrilling National Championship Final in the United States, where the very best National Show Horses compete for ribbons and thousands of dollars in prize money.

Fast Fact When it comes to National Show Horses, the flashier, the better! They come in all sorts of colours, but eye-catching palominos and pintos are especially popular.

American Cream Draft

An amazing variety of horse breeds come from North America . . . but there is only one draft breed which originated there. He's the American Cream Draft, the draft horse with a difference. And he's all the more special because he's the colour of warm cream, with amber eyes!

The first known American Cream Draft was a mare with the unflattering name of Old Granny. Her background is a mystery. All that is known is that she showed up at a farm auction in Iowa in 1911, and was purchased by a man named Harry Lakin, who was intrigued by her unique colour. Old Granny produced several foals with the same rich cream coat colour, and they all sold for above-average prices. One, a colt named Buck, became the foundation stallion for the breed, and his great-grandson, a stallion called Silver Lace, is now considered the American Cream Draft's most important sire.

To begin with, cream-coloured draft horses were bred to all sorts of other draft breeds — black and grey Percherons, sorrel Belgians, and bay Shires and Clydesdales. Only the cream-coloured foals were registered. Their numbers were never large, but a definite type began to emerge.

Today's American Cream Drafts weigh between 680 and 900 kilograms and stand 15 to 16:3 hands tall. This makes them a good, useful size for all kinds of farm work — not too big, yet strong. They are "clean-legged," meaning they don't sport the shaggy hair around their fetlocks that Clydesdales and Shires have, and their temperament, like almost all draft horses', is easy-going and willing to please.

Their colour is called "cremello" in other breeds, but American Cream Draft enthusiasts call it simply "cream": darker than white but quite a few shades lighter than palomino, with white manes and tails. They also have pink skin, and their eyes are not brown, but amber or hazel (almost orange). Not every foal born to two American Cream Draft parents inherits the cream colour, but about 80 percent do. The rest are usually chestnut with a flaxen mane and tail.

At present, there about 200 American Cream Drafts in North America, with less than a handful elsewhere in the world. But to their fans, they're the cream of the crop!

Fast Fact

As unusual as the American Cream Draft's eye colour is, it's even more startling when foals are born! Newborns have eyes that are nearly white. The eye colour starts to darken by the time they are yearlings, and is amber by the time they are mature.